MADE SIMPLE™

Cooking for Two

Publications International, Ltd.

Microwave Cooking: Microwave ovens vary in wattage. Use the cooking times as guidelines and check for doneness before adding more time.

Let's get social!
 @Publications_International
 @PublicationsInternational
www.pilbooks.com

Contents

Hearty Breakfasts

Strawberry-Topped Pancakes

Makes 2 servings

1½ cups sliced fresh strawberries

2 tablespoons seedless strawberry jam

1¼ cups all-purpose flour

¼ cup sugar

1 teaspoon baking powder

1 teaspoon baking soda

¼ teaspoon salt

1¼ cups buttermilk

1 egg, lightly beaten

1 to 2 tablespoons vegetable oil

Whipped cream (optional)

1. Combine strawberries and strawberry jam in medium bowl; stir gently to coat. Set aside while preparing pancakes.

2. Combine flour, sugar, baking powder, baking soda and salt in large bowl; mix well. Add buttermilk and egg; whisk until blended.

3. Heat 1 tablespoon oil in large skillet over medium heat or brush griddle with oil. For each pancake, pour ½ cup of batter into skillet, spreading into 5- to 6-inch circle. Cook 3 to 4 minutes or until bottom is golden brown and small bubbles appear on surface. Turn pancake; cook 2 minutes or until golden brown. Add additional oil to skillet as needed.

4. For each serving, stack three pancakes; top with strawberry mixture. Garnish with whipped cream.

Hearty Breakfasts

⅔ cup water

¼ teaspoon salt

½ cup old fashioned oats

½ cup diced apple

2 tablespoons packed brown sugar or granulated sugar

1 teaspoon vanilla

¾ teaspoon ground cinnamon

½ cup cottage cheese

¼ cup half-and-half

2 tablespoons chopped pecans or almonds

Oatmeal with Apples and Cottage Cheese

Makes 2 servings

1. Bring water and salt to a boil in small saucepan over high heat. Stir in oats, apple, brown sugar, vanilla and cinnamon. Reduce heat to medium-low; cook and stir 3 to 5 minutes or until oats are tender and creamy.

2. Stir in cottage cheese and half-and-half; spoon into serving bowls. Top with nuts.

Whole Grain French Toast

Makes 2 servings

1 egg

2 tablespoons milk

¼ teaspoon ground cinnamon

⅛ teaspoon ground nutmeg

4 slices whole wheat or multigrain bread

1 tablespoon butter

¼ cup pure maple syrup

½ cup fresh blueberries

Powdered sugar

1. Preheat oven to 400°F. Spray baking sheet with nonstick cooking spray.

2. Whisk egg, milk, cinnamon and nutmeg in shallow bowl until well blended. Dip bread slices in milk mixture, turning to coat both sides; let excess mixture drip back into bowl.

3. Melt butter in large nonstick skillet over medium heat. Add bread slices; cook 2 minutes per side or until golden brown. Transfer to prepared baking sheet. Bake 5 to 6 minutes or until heated through.

4. Microwave maple syrup in small microwavable bowl on HIGH 30 seconds or until bubbly. Stir in blueberries. Serve French toast with blueberry mixture; sprinkle with powdered sugar.

4 ounces cremini mushrooms, stems trimmed, cut into thirds

1 tablespoon olive oil, divided

½ teaspoon plus ⅛ teaspoon salt, divided

½ cup chopped onion

1 cup packed chopped stemmed lacinato kale

½ cup halved grape tomatoes

4 eggs

½ teaspoon Italian seasoning

Black pepper

⅓ cup shredded mozzarella cheese

1 tablespoon shredded Parmesan cheese

Chopped fresh parsley (optional)

Frittata Rustica

Makes 2 servings

1. Preheat oven to 400°F. Spread mushrooms on small baking sheet; drizzle with 1 teaspoon oil and sprinkle with ⅛ teaspoon salt. Roast 15 to 20 minutes or until well browned and tender.

2. Heat remaining 2 teaspoons oil in small (6- to 8-inch) ovenproof nonstick skillet over medium heat. Add onion; cook and stir 5 minutes or until soft. Add kale and ¼ teaspoon salt; cook and stir 10 minutes or until kale is tender. Add tomatoes; cook and stir 3 minutes or until tomatoes are soft. Stir in mushrooms.

3. Preheat broiler. Whisk eggs, remaining ¼ teaspoon salt, Italian seasoning and pepper in small bowl until well blended.

4. Pour egg mixture over vegetables in skillet; stir gently to mix. Cook 3 minutes or until eggs are set around edge, lifting edge to allow uncooked portion to flow underneath. Sprinkle with mozzarella and Parmesan.

5. Broil 3 minutes or until eggs are set and cheese is browned. Cut evenly into four wedges. Garnish with parsley.

1 cup pancake and
  baking mix

⅔ cup milk

1 tablespoon vegetable oil

1 egg white

  Juice of 1 lemon

2 tablespoons butter, melted

  Powdered sugar

⅔ cup assorted fresh berries
  or frozen berries, thawed

Beignet Waffles

Makes 2 servings

1. Preheat waffle maker to medium; spray lightly with nonstick cooking spray.

2. Whisk baking mix, milk, oil and egg white in large bowl until blended. Pour ¾ cup* batter into waffle maker; close and cook 4 minutes or until waffle is puffed and golden brown.

3. Remove waffle to plate; tent with foil to keep warm. Repeat with remaining batter.

4. Squeeze lemon juice over waffles. Drizzle with melted butter; top with powdered sugar and berries.

*To make irregular-shaped waffles, reduce batter to ¼ to ½ cup.

3 tablespoons butter, divided, plus additional for serving

½ cup all-purpose flour

2 tablespoons granulated sugar

¼ teaspoon salt

½ cup whole milk, at room temperature

2 eggs, at room temperature

¼ teaspoon vanilla

Powdered sugar

Lemon wedges

Dutch Baby Pancake

Makes 2 servings

1. Preheat oven to 400°F. Place 1 tablespoon butter in medium (9- to 10-inch) ovenproof skillet; place skillet in oven to heat while preparing batter. Melt remaining 2 tablespoons butter in small bowl; let cool slightly.

2. Combine flour, granulated sugar and salt in medium bowl; mix well. Add milk, eggs, 2 tablespoons melted butter and vanilla; whisk 1 minute or until batter is very smooth.

3. Remove skillet from oven; immediately pour batter into hot skillet.

4. Bake about 20 minutes or until outside of pancake is puffed and edges are deep golden brown. Sprinkle with powdered sugar; serve with lemon wedges and additional butter.

1½ cups shredded potatoes*

2 tablespoons finely chopped onion

¼ plus ⅛ teaspoon salt, divided

⅛ teaspoon black pepper

2 tablespoons butter, divided

1 tablespoon vegetable oil

½ cup diced ham (¼-inch pieces)

3 eggs

2 tablespoons milk

2 slices (1 ounce each) American cheese

Use refrigerated shredded hash brown potatoes or shredded peeled russet potatoes, squeezed dry.

Stuffed Hash Browns

Makes 2 servings

1. Preheat oven to 250°F. Place wire rack over baking sheet. Combine potatoes, onion, ¼ teaspoon salt and pepper in medium bowl; mix well.

2. Heat 1 tablespoon butter and oil in small (6- to 8-inch) nonstick skillet over medium heat. Add potato mixture; spread to cover bottom of skillet evenly, pressing down gently with spatula to flatten. Cook 10 minutes or until bottom and edges are golden brown. Cover skillet with large inverted plate; carefully flip hash browns onto plate. Slide hash browns back into skillet, cooked side up. Cook 10 minutes or until golden brown. Slide hash browns onto prepared wire rack; place in oven to keep warm while preparing ham and eggs.

3. Melt 1 teaspoon butter in same skillet over medium-high heat. Add ham; cook and stir 2 to 3 minutes or until lightly browned. Remove to plate.

4. Whisk eggs, milk and remaining ⅛ teaspoon salt in small bowl. Melt remaining 2 teaspoons butter in same skillet over medium-high heat. Add egg mixture; cook 3 minutes or just until eggs are cooked through, stirring to form large, fluffy curds. Place cheese slices on top of eggs; remove from heat and cover skillet with lid or foil to melt cheese.

5. Place hash brown on serving plate; sprinkle one side of hash brown with ham. Top ham with eggs; fold hash brown in half.

Note: Refrigerated shredded potatoes are very wet when removed from the package. For the best results, dry them well with paper towels before cooking.

½ cup thawed frozen peas

2 teaspoons lemon juice

1 teaspoon minced fresh tarragon

¼ teaspoon plus ⅛ teaspoon salt, divided

⅛ teaspoon black pepper

1 teaspoon olive oil

1 tablespoon pepitas (raw pumpkin seeds)

4 slices hearty whole grain bread, toasted

1 avocado

Avocado Toast

Makes 2 servings

1. Combine peas, lemon juice, tarragon, ¼ teaspoon salt and pepper in small food processor; pulse until blended but still chunky. Or combine all ingredients in small bowl and mash with fork to desired consistency.

2. Heat oil in small saucepan over medium heat. Add pepitas; cook and stir 1 to 2 minutes or until toasted. Transfer to small bowl; stir in remaining ⅛ teaspoon salt.

3. Spread about 1 tablespoon pea mixture over each slice of bread.

4. Cut avocado in half lengthwise around pit. Cut avocado into slices in shell; use spoon to scoop slices out of shell. Arrange avocado slices over pea mixture; top with toasted pepitas.

Hearty Breakfasts

6 eggs

¼ cup milk

2 tablespoons grated
Parmesan cheese

¼ teaspoon white or
black pepper

2 teaspoons butter

¼ cup finely chopped
red onion, divided

2 ounces smoked salmon,
cut into 1- to 2-inch
pieces

¼ cup sour cream

2 tablespoons water

2 tablespoons capers,
rinsed and drained

Finely chopped fresh
parsley (optional)

Smoked Salmon Omelet

Makes 2 servings

1. Whisk eggs, milk, cheese and pepper in small bowl until well blended.

2. Melt 1 teaspoon butter in small (6-inch) nonstick skillet over medium-high heat. Pour half of egg mixture into skillet; stir briefly. Let eggs begin to set at edges, then lift edges and tilt skillet, allowing uncooked portion of egg mixture to flow underneath. Cook 1 minute or until omelet begins to set. Sprinkle 1 tablespoon onion over half of omelet; top with half of smoked salmon. Fold other half of omelet over filling; cook 1 minute. Slide omelet onto serving plate. Repeat with remaining ingredients.

3. Whisk sour cream and water in small bowl until blended. Drizzle half over each omelet; top each with remaining 2 tablespoons onion, capers and parsley, if desired.

Strawberry Banana French Toast

Makes 2 servings

1 cup sliced fresh strawberries (about 8 medium)

2 teaspoons granulated sugar

2 eggs

½ cup milk

3 tablespoons all-purpose flour

1 teaspoon vanilla

⅛ teaspoon salt

1 tablespoon butter

4 slices (1 inch thick) egg bread or country bread

1 banana, cut into ¼-inch slices

Whipped cream and powdered sugar (optional)

Maple syrup

1. Combine strawberries and granulated sugar in small bowl; toss to coat. Set aside while preparing French toast.

2. Whisk eggs, milk, flour, vanilla and salt in shallow bowl or pie plate until well blended. Melt ½ tablespoon butter in large skillet over medium-high heat. Working with two slices at a time, dip bread into egg mixture, turning to coat completely; let excess mixture drip back into bowl. Add bread slices to skillet; cook 3 to 4 minutes per side or until golden brown. Repeat with remaining butter and bread slices.

3. Top each serving with strawberry mixture and banana slices. Garnish with whipped cream and powdered sugar; serve with maple syrup.

Hearty Breakfasts

½ cup uncooked quinoa

1 cup water

1 tablespoon packed brown sugar

2 teaspoons maple syrup

½ teaspoon ground cinnamon

¼ cup golden raisins (optional)

Milk (optional)

¼ cup fresh raspberries

½ banana, sliced

Breakfast Quinoa

Makes 2 servings

1. Place quinoa in fine-mesh strainer; rinse well under cold water. Transfer to small saucepan.

2. Stir in 1 cup water, brown sugar, maple syrup and cinnamon; bring to a boil over high heat. Reduce heat to low; cover and simmer 10 to 15 minutes or until quinoa is tender and water is absorbed. Add raisins, if desired, during last 5 minutes of cooking.

3. Serve with milk, if desired; top with raspberries and banana.

Hearty Breakfasts

Turkey and Bacon Mini Wafflewiches

Makes 2 servings

1 teaspoon Dijon mustard

1 teaspoon honey

8 frozen mini waffles
   (2 pieces, divided into
   individual waffles)

2 thin slices deli turkey,
   cut into thin strips

2 tablespoons crumbled
   cooked bacon

2 tablespoons shredded
   Cheddar or
   mozzarella cheese

2 teaspoons butter

1. Combine mustard and honey in small bowl; mix well. Spread small amount of mustard mixture on one side of four waffles. Top with turkey, bacon, cheese and remaining waffles.

2. Melt butter in medium nonstick skillet over medium heat. Cook sandwiches 3 to 4 minutes per side or until cheese is melted and waffles are golden brown, pressing down with back of spatula.

Satisfying Soups

Acorn Squash Soup with Chicken and Red Pepper Meatballs

Makes 2 servings

1 small to medium acorn squash (about 12 ounces)

8 ounces ground chicken or turkey

1 red bell pepper, seeded and finely chopped

1 egg

1 teaspoon dried parsley flakes

1 teaspoon ground coriander

½ teaspoon black pepper

¼ teaspoon salt

¼ teaspoon ground cinnamon

3 cups vegetable broth

2 tablespoons sour cream (optional)

Ground red pepper (optional)

1. Pierce squash skin with fork. Place in microwavable dish; microwave on HIGH 8 to 10 minutes or until tender. Cool 10 minutes.

2. Meanwhile, combine chicken, bell pepper, egg, parsley flakes, coriander, black pepper, salt and cinnamon in large bowl; mix lightly. Shape mixture into eight meatballs. Place meatballs in microwavable dish; microwave on HIGH 5 minutes or until cooked through. Set aside to cool.

3. Remove and discard seeds from cooled squash. Scrape squash flesh from shell into large saucepan; mash squash with potato masher. Add broth and meatballs to saucepan; cook over medium-high heat 12 minutes, stirring occasionally. Add additional liquid if necessary.

4. Garnish each serving with 1 tablespoon sour cream and ground red pepper.

French Onion Soup for Deux

Makes 2 servings

1 tablespoon olive oil

12 ounces yellow onions, halved lengthwise and cut into thin strips

1 clove garlic, thinly sliced

¼ teaspoon salt

¼ teaspoon black pepper

1 cup chicken broth

1 cup water

1 tablespoon balsamic vinegar

1 bay leaf

½ teaspoon dried thyme

2 thick slices crusty, peasant-style bread

¼ cup (1 ounce) shredded white cheese, such as Muenster or Monterey Jack

1. Heat oil in large saucepan over medium heat. Add onions and garlic; cook 20 minutes or until onions are soft and golden brown, stirring frequently. If onions begin to stick or burn, reduce heat slightly and add water, one tablespoon at a time. Sprinkle onions with salt and pepper.

2. Add broth, water, vinegar, bay leaf and thyme; cook over low heat until heated through. Remove and discard bay leaf.

3. Preheat broiler. Toast bread under broiler on both sides.

4. To serve, ladle soup into two ovenproof bowls; top each with toasted bread. Sprinkle bread with cheese. Place bowls on baking sheet; broil until cheese melts and is bubbly and browned.

New England Clam Chowder

Makes 2 servings

1 can (5 ounces) whole baby clams, undrained

1 baking potato, peeled and coarsely chopped

¼ cup finely chopped onion

⅔ cup evaporated milk

¼ teaspoon salt

¼ teaspoon white pepper

¼ teaspoon dried thyme

1 tablespoon butter

1. Drain clams, reserving juice. Add enough water to reserved juice to measure ⅔ cup.

2. Combine clam juice mixture, potato and onion in medium saucepan; bring to a boil over high heat. Reduce heat to low; cook 8 minutes or until potato is tender.

3. Add evaporated milk, salt, pepper and thyme to saucepan; cook and stir 2 minutes over medium-high heat. Add butter; cook 5 minutes or until soup thickens, stirring occasionally.

4. Add clams; cook 5 minutes or until clams are firm, stirring occasionally.

Satisfying Soups

1 tablespoon olive oil

1 small onion, chopped

1¼ cups chicken broth

1 cup thinly sliced carrots

½ teaspoon Italian seasoning

¼ teaspoon salt

1 can (about 14 ounces) diced tomatoes

1 cup diced cooked chicken breast

3 cups sliced kale or baby spinach

Chunky Chicken Soup

Makes 2 servings

1. Heat oil in large saucepan over medium-high heat. Add onion; cook and stir about 5 minutes or until golden brown. Stir in broth, carrots, Italian seasoning and salt; bring to a boil. Reduce heat to low; cook 5 minutes.

2. Stir in tomatoes; cook over medium heat 5 minutes or until carrots are tender. Add chicken; cook and stir 3 minutes or until heated through. Add kale; cook and stir until wilted.

Satisfying Soups

2 teaspoons olive oil

½ cup finely chopped onion

1 cup chicken broth

3 cups small broccoli florets or thawed frozen chopped broccoli

½ cup evaporated milk

⅛ teaspoon ground red pepper

2 ounces cubed pasteurized process cheese product

¼ cup sour cream

⅛ teaspoon salt

Cheesy Broccoli Soup

Makes 2 servings

1. Heat oil in medium saucepan over medium-high heat. Add onion; cook and stir 4 minutes or until translucent.

2. Stir in broth; bring to a boil over high heat. Add broccoli; return to a boil. Reduce heat to low; cover and cook 5 minutes or until broccoli is tender.

3. Whisk in evaporated milk and red pepper. Remove from heat; stir in cheese product until melted. Stir in sour cream and salt.

2 cans (about 14 ounces each) chicken broth

1 tablespoon soy sauce

2 teaspoons cornstarch

2 eggs, beaten

¼ cup thinly sliced green onions

Egg Drop Soup

Makes 2 servings

1. Bring broth to a boil in large saucepan over high heat. Reduce heat to medium-low.

2. Stir soy sauce and cornstarch in small bowl until smooth and well blended; stir into broth. Cook and stir 2 minutes or until slightly thickened.

3. Stirring constantly in one direction, slowly pour eggs into soup in thin, steady stream.

4. Ladle soup into bowls; sprinkle with green onions.

Shrimp Gazpacho

Makes 2 servings

- 1 tablespoon olive oil
- 8 ounces medium shrimp, peeled and deveined (with tails on)
- ¼ teaspoon salt
- ⅛ teaspoon black pepper
- 3 plum tomatoes, chopped (about 1½ cups)
- ¼ small red onion, chopped
- 1 clove garlic, chopped
- ¼ cucumber, peeled and chopped
- ¼ cup finely chopped jarred roasted red peppers, divided
- ¾ cup tomato juice
- 1 tablespoon red wine vinegar

1. Heat oil in medium nonstick skillet over high heat. Season shrimp with salt and black pepper. Add to skillet; cook 3 minutes or until browned on both sides and opaque in center. Remove to plate.

2. Combine tomatoes, onion, garlic, cucumber and half of roasted peppers in food processor; process until blended. Add tomato juice and vinegar; process until smooth.

3. Divide tomato mixture among bowls; top with shrimp and remaining roasted peppers.

French Peasant Soup

Makes 2 servings

1 slice bacon, chopped

½ cup diced carrot

½ cup diced celery

¼ cup minced onion

1 clove garlic, minced

2 tablespoons dry white
wine or water

1 can (about 14 ounces)
vegetable broth

1 bay leaf

1 sprig fresh thyme *or*
1 teaspoon dried thyme

1 sprig fresh parsley *or*
1 teaspoon dried
parsley flakes

½ cup chopped green beans
(½-inch pieces)

2 tablespoons uncooked
small pasta or elbow
macaroni

½ cup canned cannellini
beans, rinsed and drained

½ cup diced zucchini

¼ cup chopped leek

2 teaspoons prepared pesto

Grated Parmesan cheese

1. Cook bacon in medium saucepan over medium heat 3 minutes or until partially cooked.

2. Add carrot, celery, onion and garlic to saucepan; cook 5 minutes or until carrots are crisp-tender, stirring occasionally. Add wine; cook until most of wine has evaporated. Add broth, bay leaf, thyme and parsley; cook 10 minutes.

3. Add green beans to saucepan; cook 5 minutes. Add pasta; cook 5 to 7 minutes or until almost tender. Add cannellini beans, zucchini and leek; cook 3 to 5 minutes or until vegetables are tender.

4. Remove and discard bay leaf and herb sprigs. Ladle soup into two bowls. Stir 1 teaspoon pesto into each bowl; sprinkle with cheese.

Simple Seafood

Salmon-Potato Cakes with Mustard Tartar Sauce

Makes 2 servings

- 3 small unpeeled red potatoes (8 ounces), halved
- 1 cup water
- 1 cup flaked cooked salmon
- 2 green onions, chopped
- 1 egg white
- 2 tablespoons chopped fresh parsley, divided
- ½ teaspoon Cajun or Creole seasoning mix
- 1 tablespoon olive or canola oil
- 1 tablespoon mayonnaise
- 1 tablespoon plain yogurt or sour cream
- 2 teaspoons coarse-grain mustard
- 1 tablespoon chopped dill pickle
- 1 teaspoon lemon juice

1. Combine potatoes and water in medium saucepan; bring to a boil over high heat. Reduce heat to low; cook about 15 minutes or until potatoes are tender. Drain potatoes; transfer to medium bowl. Mash potatoes with fork, leaving chunky texture.

2. Add salmon, green onions, egg white, 1 tablespoon parsley and Cajun seasoning to potatoes; stir until blended. Gently shape salmon mixture into two patties.

3. Heat oil in medium nonstick skillet over medium heat. Place patties in skillet; flatten slightly. Cook 3 to 4 minutes per side or until browned and heated through.

4. Meanwhile, combine mayonnaise, yogurt, mustard, remaining 1 tablespoon parsley, pickle and lemon juice in small bowl; mix well. Serve sauce with cakes.

Tuna Steaks with Pineapple and Tomato Salsa

Makes 2 servings

1 medium tomato, chopped

1 can (8 ounces) pineapple chunks in juice, drained and chopped

1 tablespoon chopped fresh cilantro

1 jalapeño pepper, seeded and minced

1½ teaspoons minced red onion

1 teaspoon lime juice

¼ teaspoon grated lime peel

2 tuna steaks (about 4 ounces each)

¼ teaspoon salt

⅛ teaspoon black pepper

2 teaspoons olive oil

1. For salsa, combine tomato, pineapple, cilantro, jalapeño, onion, lime juice and lime peel in medium bowl; mix well.

2. Sprinkle tuna with salt and black pepper. Heat oil in large skillet over medium-high heat. Add tuna; cook 2 to 3 minutes per side for medium rare or to desired doneness. Serve with salsa.

Roasted Almond Tilapia

Makes 2 servings

- 2 tilapia or Boston scrod fillets (6 ounces each)
- ¼ teaspoon salt
- 1 tablespoon prepared mustard
- ¼ cup whole wheat bread crumbs
- 2 tablespoons chopped almonds
- Paprika (optional)
- Lemon wedges (optional)

1. Preheat oven to 450°F. Place tilapia on small baking sheet; season with salt. Spread mustard over fish.

2. Combine bread crumbs and almonds in small bowl; mix well. Sprinkle over tilapia, pressing lightly to adhere. Sprinkle with paprika, if desired.

3. Bake 8 to 10 minutes or until fish begins to flake when tested with fork. Serve with lemon wedges, if desired.

Pan-Cooked
Bok Choy Salmon

Makes 2 servings

1 pound bok choy or Napa
  cabbage, chopped

1 cup broccoli slaw mix

2 tablespoons olive oil,
  divided

2 salmon fillets (4 to
  6 ounces each)

¼ teaspoon salt

½ teaspoon black pepper

1 teaspoon sesame seeds

1. Combine bok choy and broccoli slaw mix in colander; rinse and drain well.

2. Heat 1 tablespoon oil in large skillet over medium heat. Sprinkle salmon with salt and pepper. Add to skillet; cook 3 minutes per side. Remove to plate.

3. Add remaining 1 tablespoon oil and sesame seeds to skillet; stir to toast sesame seeds. Add bok choy mixture; cook and stir 3 to 4 minutes.

4. Return salmon to skillet. Reduce heat to low; cover and cook 4 minutes or until fish begins to flake when tested with fork.

Baked Orange Roughy with Sautéed Vegetables

Makes 2 servings

2 orange roughy fillets (about 4 ounces each)

2 teaspoons olive oil

1 medium carrot, cut into matchstick-size pieces

4 medium mushrooms, sliced

⅓ cup chopped onion

¼ cup chopped green or yellow bell pepper

1 clove garlic, minced

Black pepper

Lemon wedges

1. Preheat oven to 350°F. Place orange roughy in shallow baking dish. Bake 15 minutes or until fish begins to flake when tested with fork.

2. Heat oil in medium skillet over medium-high heat. Add carrot; cook 3 minutes, stirring occasionally. Add mushrooms, onion, bell pepper and garlic; cook and stir 3 minutes or until vegetables are crisp-tender.

3. Place orange roughy on serving plates; top with vegetable mixture. Sprinkle with black pepper. Serve with lemon wedges.

Note: To broil fish, place orange roughy on rack of broiler pan. Broil 4 to 6 inches from heat 4 minutes per side or until fish begins to flake when tested with fork.

Shrimp and Soba Noodle Salad

Makes 2 servings

4 ounces soba noodles, cooked and well drained

1 package (12 ounces) medium shrimp, cooked, peeled and well drained*

2 cups coarsely chopped broccoli florets, cooked until crisp-tender and drained

¼ cup minced green onions

2 tablespoons soy sauce

2 tablespoons chili-garlic sauce

1 tablespoon canola or sesame oil

½ teaspoon grated fresh ginger

1 tablespoon lightly toasted sesame seeds** (optional)

Or use 1 package (12 ounces) frozen peeled cooked baby shrimp. Drain well, squeezing out excess moisture before adding to salad.

**To toast sesame seeds, cook and stir in small skillet over medium heat 2 minutes or until seeds begin to pop and turn golden brown.*

1. Combine noodles, shrimp, broccoli and green onions in large serving bowl.

2. Whisk soy sauce, chili-garlic sauce, oil and ginger in small bowl until well blended. Pour over noodle mixture; toss gently to coat. Let stand 10 minutes for flavors to blend. Garnish with sesame seeds.

Teriyaki Salmon with Asian Slaw

Makes 2 servings

3 tablespoons teriyaki sauce, divided

2 salmon fillets with skin (about 4 to 5 ounces each and 1 inch thick)

2½ cups coleslaw mix

1 cup snow peas, cut into thin strips

½ cup thinly sliced radishes

2 tablespoons orange marmalade

1 teaspoon dark sesame oil

1. Preheat broiler or prepare grill for direct cooking. Spoon 1½ tablespoons teriyaki sauce over fleshy sides of salmon. Let stand while preparing vegetable mixture.

2. Combine coleslaw mix, snow peas and radishes in large bowl. Combine remaining 1½ tablespoons teriyaki sauce, marmalade and oil in small bowl; mix well. Add to coleslaw mixture; toss to coat.

3. Broil salmon 4 to 5 inches from heat source, or grill, flesh side down, over medium heat 6 to 10 minutes or until center is opaque and fish begins to flake when tested with fork.

4. Transfer coleslaw mixture to serving plates; serve with salmon.

Niçoise Salad Wraps

Makes 2 servings

½ cup chopped green beans (½-inch pieces)

2 new red potatoes, each cut into 8 wedges

3 tablespoons Italian vinaigrette, divided

1 egg

2 cups watercress leaves

4 ounces albacore tuna, drained and flaked (about ½ cup)

8 niçoise olives, pitted and halved

3 cherry tomatoes, quartered

2 (10-inch) whole wheat tortillas

1. Bring 8 cups water to a boil in large saucepan over high heat. Add green beans and potatoes; cook over low heat 6 minutes or until tender. Use slotted spoon to remove vegetables to bowl of ice water to stop cooking; drain on paper towels. Transfer to medium bowl; toss with half of vinaigrette.

2. Bring water back to a boil. Add egg; cook over low heat 12 minutes. Remove to bowl of ice water. When cool enough to handle, peel egg and cut into eight wedges.

3. Add watercress, tuna, olives, tomatoes and remaining vinaigrette to bowl with vegetables; toss gently to coat.

4. Heat tortillas in nonstick skillet over medium-high heat, turning when softened. Place on plates. Divide salad between tortillas; top with egg wedges. Roll up tortillas to enclose filling. Cut wraps diagonally into halves before serving.

Tuna Salad Sandwich

Makes 2 servings

1 can (12 ounces) solid white albacore tuna, drained

1 can (5 ounces) chunk white albacore tuna, drained

¼ cup mayonnaise

1 tablespoon pickle relish

2 teaspoons spicy brown mustard

1 teaspoon lemon juice

½ teaspoon salt

¼ teaspoon black pepper

2 pieces focaccia (about 4×3 inches), split and toasted *or* 4 slices honey wheat bread

Lettuce, tomato and red onion slices

1. Place tuna in medium bowl; flake with fork. Add mayonnaise, pickle relish, mustard, lemon juice, salt and pepper; mix well.

2. Serve tuna salad on focaccia with lettuce, tomato and onion.

Grilled Salmon Salad with Orange-Basil Vinaigrette

Makes 2 servings

¼ cup frozen orange juice
concentrate, thawed

1½ tablespoons white wine
vinegar or cider vinegar

1 tablespoon chopped
fresh basil *or* 1 teaspoon
dried basil

1½ teaspoons olive oil

1 salmon fillet (about
8 ounces)

4 cups torn mixed greens

¾ cup sliced strawberries

10 to 12 thin cucumber slices,
cut into halves

⅛ teaspoon black pepper

1. Whisk orange juice concentrate, vinegar, basil and oil in small bowl until well blended. Remove 2 tablespoons orange juice mixture; reserve remaining mixture to use as salad dressing.

2. Prepare grill for direct cooking. Spray grid with nonstick cooking spray.

3. Grill salmon, skin side down, over medium heat 5 minutes. Turn and grill 5 minutes or until fish begins to flake when tested with fork, brushing frequently with 2 tablespoons orange juice mixture. Cool slightly.

4. Combine greens, strawberries and cucumber in large bowl; toss gently. Place on two serving plates.

5. Remove skin from salmon. Break salmon into chunks; arrange over greens. Drizzle with reserved orange juice mixture; sprinkle with pepper.

Chicken & Turkey

Chicken & Turkey

4 skinless chicken
   drumsticks
   (about 1 pound)

¼ cup barbecue sauce

¼ cup raspberry fruit spread

½ teaspoon grated orange
   peel

⅛ teaspoon ground allspice

   Pinch red pepper flakes

Raspberry-Orange BBQ Drums

Makes 2 servings

1. Preheat broiler. Lightly spray broiler rack and pan with nonstick cooking spray. Arrange drumsticks on rack.

2. Broil drumsticks 25 minutes, turning every 5 minutes.

3. Combine barbecue sauce, fruit spread, orange peel, allspice and red pepper flakes in small bowl; mix well.

4. Brush half of sauce mixture over chicken; broil 1 minute. Turn and brush with remaining sauce; broil 1 minute.

½ cup panko bread crumbs

3 teaspoons assorted dried herbs (such as rosemary, basil, parsley, thyme or oregano), divided

Salt and black pepper

2 tablespoons mayonnaise

2 boneless skinless chicken breasts (about 4 ounces each)

Baked Panko Chicken

Makes 2 servings

1. Preheat oven to 375°F. Line baking sheet with parchment paper; spray with nonstick cooking spray.

2. Combine panko, 1 teaspoon herbs, salt and pepper on shallow plate. Combine mayonnaise and remaining 2 teaspoons herbs in small bowl; mix well.

3. Spread mayonnaise mixture over chicken. Coat chicken with panko mixture, pressing to adhere. Place chicken on prepared baking sheet.

4. Bake 30 to 35 minutes or until chicken is no longer pink in center.

Grilled Salsa Turkey Burger

Makes 2 servings

8 ounces ground turkey

2 tablespoons mild or medium salsa, plus additional for serving

2 tablespoons crushed baked tortilla chips

2 slices (1 ounce each) Monterey Jack cheese

2 whole wheat hamburger buns, split

Green leaf lettuce

1. Prepare grill for direct cooking. Spray grid with nonstick cooking spray.

2. Combine turkey, 2 tablespoons salsa and chips in small bowl; mix lightly. Shape into two patties.

3. Grill patties over medium-high heat about 6 minutes per side or until cooked through (165°F). Top with cheese during last 2 minutes of grilling. Toast buns on grill, cut sides down, during last 2 minutes of grilling.

4. Place lettuce on bottom halves of buns; top with burgers, additional salsa, if desired, and top halves of buns.

Note: To broil burgers, preheat broiler. Broil patties 4 to 6 inches from heat 6 minutes per side or until cooked through (165°F).

Sweet and Sour Chicken

Makes 2 servings

- 1 tablespoon unseasoned rice vinegar
- 1 tablespoon soy sauce
- 2 cloves garlic, minced
- ¼ teaspoon minced fresh ginger
- ⅛ teaspoon red pepper flakes (optional)
- 3 ounces boneless skinless chicken breasts, cut into ½-inch strips
- 1 teaspoon vegetable oil
- 2 green onions, cut into 1-inch pieces
- 1 green bell pepper, cut into 1-inch pieces
- 1½ teaspoons cornstarch
- ¼ cup chicken broth
- 1 tablespoon apricot fruit spread
- 1 can (11 ounces) mandarin orange segments, drained
- 1 cup hot cooked rice

1. Whisk vinegar, soy sauce, garlic, ginger and red pepper flakes, if desired, in medium bowl until well blended. Add chicken; toss to coat. Marinate 20 minutes at room temperature.

2. Heat oil in wok or large nonstick skillet over medium heat. Drain chicken; reserve marinade. Add chicken to wok; stir-fry 3 minutes. Stir in green onions and bell pepper.

3. Stir cornstarch into reserved marinade until well blended. Stir broth, fruit spread and marinade mixture into wok. Bring to a boil; cook and stir 2 minutes or until chicken is cooked through and sauce is thickened. Add mandarin oranges; cook until heated through. Serve over rice.

Lime-Mustard Marinated Chicken

Makes 2 servings

2 boneless skinless chicken breasts (about 4 ounces each)

¼ cup lime juice

3 tablespoons honey mustard, divided

1 tablespoon olive oil

½ teaspoon salt, divided

¼ teaspoon ground cumin

⅛ teaspoon garlic powder

⅛ teaspoon ground red pepper

¾ cup plus 2 tablespoons chicken broth, divided

¼ cup uncooked rice

1 cup broccoli florets

⅓ cup matchstick carrots

1. Place chicken in large resealable food storage bag. Whisk lime juice, 2 tablespoons mustard, oil, ¼ teaspoon salt, cumin, garlic powder and red pepper in small bowl until well blended. Pour mixture over chicken. Seal bag; turn to coat. Marinate in refrigerator 2 hours.

2. Combine ¾ cup broth, rice and remaining 1 tablespoon mustard and ¼ teaspoon salt in small saucepan; bring to a boil over high heat. Reduce heat to medium; cover and simmer 12 minutes or until rice is almost tender.

3. Stir in broccoli, carrots and remaining 2 tablespoons broth; cover and cook 2 to 3 minutes or until vegetables are crisp-tender and rice is tender.

4. Meanwhile, prepare grill for direct cooking. Remove chicken from marinade; discard marinade.

5. Grill chicken, covered, over medium heat 5 to 6 minutes per side or until no longer pink in center. Serve with rice mixture.

Chicken and Avocado Overstuffed Quesadillas

Makes 2 servings

3 tablespoons Caesar dressing

2 teaspoons finely chopped fresh cilantro

2 burrito-size flour tortillas (10 to 11 inches)

¾ cup (3 ounces) shredded Monterey Jack cheese, divided

1 cup chopped grilled chicken strips (¾-inch pieces)

½ cup shredded green cabbage

½ cup pico de gallo

1 avocado, sliced

2 tablespoons vegetable oil

1. Combine dressing and cilantro in small bowl; mix well. Roll up tortillas in paper towel or waxed paper; microwave on HIGH 10 seconds or until softened.

2. Place tortillas on work surface. For each quesadilla, sprinkle ¼ cup cheese in circle in center of tortilla, leaving 3-inch border all around. Top with half of chicken; drizzle with half of dressing mixture. Top with half each of cabbage, pico de gallo and avocado; sprinkle with 2 tablespoons cheese.

3. Working with one tortilla at a time, fold top of tortilla down over filling to center. Hold folded part down while working in clockwise direction, folding next section of tortilla in towards center until filling is completely covered. (You should end up with five folds and a hexagonal shape. If there is an uncovered hole in center of tortilla after folding, cut round piece from another tortilla to cover it.)

4. Heat 1 tablespoon oil in medium nonstick skillet over medium heat. Cook quesadilla, folded side down, about 5 minutes or until golden brown, pressing down with spatula. Turn and cook 4 to 5 minutes or until top is golden brown. Repeat with remaining 1 tablespoon oil and quesadilla.

Spiced Turkey with Fruit Salsa

Makes 2 servings

1 turkey breast tenderloin (about 6 ounces)

2 teaspoons lime juice

1 teaspoon mesquite seasoning blend or ground cumin

½ cup frozen pitted sweet cherries, thawed and halved*

¼ cup chunky salsa

Drained canned sweet cherries can be substituted for frozen cherries.

1. Prepare grill for direct cooking. Brush turkey with lime juice; sprinkle with mesquite seasoning.

2. Grill turkey, covered, over medium heat 15 to 20 minutes or until cooked through (165°F).

3. Meanwhile, combine cherries and salsa in small bowl; mix well. Thinly slice turkey; serve with salsa mixture.

1 tablespoon butter

1 boneless skinless chicken
breast, cut into strips
(about 4 ounces)

1 package (5 ounces) long
grain and wild rice mix
with seasoning

1 cup water

6 dried apricots, cut into
slivers

Chicken and Wild Rice
Skillet Dinner

Makes 2 servings

1. Melt butter in medium skillet over medium-high heat. Add chicken; cook and stir 3 to 4 minutes or until lightly browned.

2. Meanwhile, measure ½ cup rice and 2 tablespoons seasoning mix from package. (Reserve remaining rice and seasoning mix for another use.)

3. Add rice, seasoning mix, water and apricots to skillet; bring to a boil. Reduce heat to low; cover and cook 25 minutes or until liquid is absorbed and rice is tender.

2 (6- to 7-inch) round
   flatbreads or Greek-style
   pita bread rounds
   (no pocket)

2 tablespoons prepared
   pesto

1 cup grilled chicken strips

4 slices (1 ounce each)
   mozzarella cheese

1 plum tomato, cut into
   ¼-inch slices

3 tablespoons shredded
   Parmesan cheese

Chicken Pesto Flatbreads

Makes 2 servings

1. Place flatbreads on work surface. Spread 1 tablespoon pesto over half of each flatbread. Place chicken on opposite half of bread; top with mozzarella, tomato and Parmesan. Fold pesto-topped bread half over filling.

2. Spray grill pan or nonstick skillet with nonstick cooking spray or brush with vegetable oil; heat over medium-high heat. Cook sandwiches 3 minutes per side or until bread is toasted, cheese begins to melt and sandwiches are heated through.

Chicken & Turkey

2 boneless skinless chicken breasts (about 4 ounces each)

¼ cup mayonnaise or salad dressing, plus additional for serving

½ teaspoon black pepper

4 large lettuce leaves

1 large tomato, seeded and diced

3 slices bacon, crisp-cooked and crumbled

1 hard-cooked egg, chopped

BLT Chicken Salad for Two

Makes 2 servings

1. Prepare grill for direct cooking.

2. Brush chicken with ¼ cup mayonnaise; sprinkle with pepper. Grill over medium heat 5 to 7 minutes per side or until no longer pink in center. Cool slightly; cut into thin slices.

3. Arrange lettuce on serving plates; top with chicken, tomato, bacon and egg. Serve with additional mayonnaise, if desired.

Chicken & Turkey

Bacon Jam

- 1 pound thick-cut bacon, chopped
- 2 large onions, chopped (about 1 pound)
- ⅓ cup packed brown sugar
- ⅛ teaspoon red pepper flakes
- ⅔ cup water
- ¼ cup coffee
- 1½ tablespoons balsamic vinegar

Garlic Aioli

- ¼ cup mayonnaise
- 1 clove garlic, minced
- 1 teaspoon lemon juice
- ⅛ teaspoon salt

Panini

- 2 (6- to 7-inch) round focaccia breads, split
- 2 plum tomatoes, cut into ¼-inch slices
- 6 ounces sliced fresh mozzarella (¼-inch-thick slices)
- 6 ounces thickly sliced turkey breast (about ¼-inch-thick slices)
- ½ cup baby arugula

Turkey Mozzarella Panini

Makes 2 servings

1. For bacon jam, cook bacon in large skillet over medium-high heat 10 to 15 minutes or until bacon is cooked through but still chewy (not crisp), stirring occasionally. Remove bacon to paper towel-lined plate. Drain off all but 1 tablespoon drippings from skillet.

2. Add onions to skillet; cook 10 minutes, stirring occasionally. Add brown sugar and red pepper flakes; cook over medium-low heat 18 to 20 minutes or until onions are deep golden brown. Stir in bacon, water and coffee; cook over medium heat 25 minutes or until mixture is thick and jammy, stirring occasionally. Stir in vinegar.*

3. For garlic aioli, combine mayonnaise, garlic, lemon juice and salt in small bowl; mix well.

4. Spread bottom halves of focaccia with garlic aioli. Top with tomatoes, cheese, turkey and arugula. Spread top halves of focaccia with bacon jam; place over arugula. Serve immediately.

Recipe makes about 1½ cups bacon jam. Store remaining jam in refrigerator up to 2 weeks; return to room temperature before serving.

Grilled Chicken with Spicy Black Beans and Rice

Makes 2 servings

- 2 boneless skinless chicken breasts (about 4 ounces each)
- 1 teaspoon Caribbean jerk seasoning
- 2 teaspoons olive oil
- ¼ cup finely diced green bell pepper
- 2 teaspoons chipotle chili powder
- 1 cup hot cooked rice
- ½ cup canned black beans, rinsed and drained
- 2 tablespoons diced pimientos
- 2 tablespoons chopped pimiento-stuffed green olives
- 1 tablespoon chopped onion
- 1 tablespoon chopped fresh cilantro (optional)

  Lime wedges

1. Prepare grill for direct cooking. Spray grid with nonstick cooking spray.

2. Rub chicken with jerk seasoning. Grill over medium heat about 5 minutes per side or until no longer pink in center.

3. Meanwhile, heat oil in medium saucepan or skillet over medium heat. Add bell pepper and chili powder; cook and stir about 3 minutes or until tender.

4. Add rice, beans, pimientos and olives to saucepan; cook about 3 minutes or until heated through.

5. Slice chicken; serve with rice mixture. Sprinkle with onion and cilantro, if desired. Serve with lime wedges.

Beef & Pork

1 beef flank steak
(about 1 pound)

1 tablespoon soy sauce

1 tablespoon hoisin sauce

1½ teaspoons dark sesame oil

1 clove garlic, minced

Sesame-Garlic Flank Steak

Makes 2 servings

1. Score steak lightly with sharp knife in diamond pattern on both sides; place in large resealable food storage bag.

2. Combine soy sauce, hoisin sauce, oil and garlic in small bowl; pour over steak. Seal bag; turn to coat. Marinate in refrigerator at least 2 hours or up to 24 hours, turning once.

3. Prepare grill for direct cooking. Remove steak from marinade; reserve marinade.

4. Grill steak, covered, over medium heat 13 to 18 minutes for medium rare (145°F) or to desired doneness, turning and brushing with marinade halfway through cooking time. Discard remaining marinade. Remove steak to cutting board; let rest 5 minutes. Cut into thin slices across the grain.

Fiesta Beef Enchiladas

Makes 2 servings

6 ounces ground beef

¼ cup sliced green onions

1 teaspoon minced garlic

½ cup mild or hot red or green enchilada sauce

1 cup (4 ounces) shredded Mexican cheese blend or Cheddar cheese, divided

¾ cup chopped tomato, divided

½ cup frozen corn, thawed

½ cup cooked black beans

⅓ cup cooked white or brown rice

¼ cup salsa or picante sauce

6 (6-inch) corn tortillas

2 sheets (20×12 inches each) heavy-duty foil, generously sprayed with nonstick cooking spray

½ cup sliced romaine lettuce

1. Preheat oven to 375°F. Cook ground beef in large skillet over medium-high heat 6 to 8 minutes or until browned, stirring to break up meat. Drain fat. Add green onions and garlic; cook and stir 2 minutes.

2. Combine beef mixture, enchilada sauce, ¾ cup cheese, ½ cup tomato, corn, beans, rice and salsa in large bowl; mix well. Spoon mixture down center of tortillas. Roll up tortillas and filling; place three enchiladas, seam side down, on each foil sheet.

3. Double fold sides and ends of foil to seal packets, leaving head space for heat circulation. Place packets on large baking sheet.

4. Bake 15 minutes. Remove from oven; open packets. Sprinkle with remaining ¼ cup cheese; reseal packets. Bake 10 minutes or until cheese is melted. Serve with lettuce and remaining ¼ cup tomato.

Apple-Cherry Glazed Pork Chops

Makes 2 servings

½ teaspoon salt

½ teaspoon dried thyme

⅛ teaspoon black pepper

2 boneless pork loin chops
(4 ounces each), trimmed

2 teaspoons vegetable oil

⅔ cup unsweetened
apple juice

½ medium apple, sliced

2 tablespoons sliced
green onion

2 tablespoons dried
tart cherries

1 teaspoon cornstarch

1 tablespoon water

1. Combine salt, thyme and pepper in small bowl; mix well. Rub onto both sides of pork chops.

2. Heat oil in large skillet over medium heat. Add pork; cook about 2 minutes per side or until barely pink in center, turning once. Remove to plate; tent with foil to keep warm.

3. Add apple juice, apple slices, green onion and cherries to skillet; cook over medium heat 2 to 3 minutes or until apple and green onion are tender.

4. Stir cornstarch into water in small bowl until smooth; add to skillet. Bring to a boil; cook and stir until thickened. Spoon apple mixture over pork chops.

1½ cups (3 ounces) uncooked
   wagon wheel pasta

3 ounces ground beef

2 tablespoons chopped
   onion

2 tablespoons chopped
   green bell pepper

1 clove garlic, minced

½ cup pasta sauce

   Dash black pepper

¼ cup (1 ounce) shredded
   Italian cheese blend

Baked Pasta Casserole

Makes 2 servings

1. Preheat oven to 350°F. Cook pasta according to package directions; drain and return to saucepan.

2. Meanwhile, cook beef, onion, bell pepper and garlic in medium skillet over medium-high heat 3 to 4 minutes or until beef is no longer pink and vegetables are crisp-tender, stirring frequently. Drain fat.

3. Add beef mixture, pasta sauce and black pepper to pasta in saucepan; stir to coat. Spoon mixture into 1-quart baking dish. Sprinkle with cheese.

4. Bake 15 minutes or until heated through.

Note: *To make ahead, assemble casserole as directed above through step 3. Cover and refrigerate several hours or overnight. Bake, uncovered, in preheated 350°F oven 30 minutes or until heated through.*

Beef & Pork

8   ounces boneless beef
     top sirloin steak, cut
     into 1-inch cubes

1   medium red potato,
     peeled and cut into
     ¾-inch pieces

1   cup frozen mixed
     vegetables

⅔   cup beef gravy

½   teaspoon dried
     parsley flakes

¼   teaspoon salt

¼   teaspoon dried thyme

⅛   teaspoon black pepper

1   sheet (20×12 inches)
     heavy-duty foil, lightly
     sprayed with nonstick
     cooking spray

Quick Beef Stew in Foil

Makes 2 servings

1. Preheat oven to 450°F.

2. Combine beef, potato, mixed vegetables, gravy parsley flakes, salt, thyme and pepper in medium bowl; mix well.

3. Place beef mixture in center of foil sheet. Double fold sides and ends of foil to seal packet, leaving head space for heat circulation. Place packet on baking sheet.

4. Bake 30 minutes or until beef is tender. Carefully open one end of packet to allow steam to escape. Open packet and transfer stew to two bowls.

Beef & Pork

2 teaspoons vegetable oil

8 ounces pork tenderloin, cut into ½-inch strips

4 green onions, cut into ½-inch pieces

1½ cups coleslaw mix

2 tablespoons hoisin sauce or Asian plum sauce

4 (8-inch) flour tortillas, warmed

Easy Moo Shu Pork

Makes 2 servings

1. Heat oil in large skillet over medium-high heat. Add pork and green onions; stir-fry 2 to 3 minutes or until pork is barely pink in center. Stir in coleslaw mix and hoisin sauce.

2. Spoon pork mixture onto tortillas. Roll up tortillas, folding in sides to enclose filling.

Note: *To heat tortillas, stack and wrap loosely in plastic wrap. Microwave on HIGH 15 to 20 seconds or until warm and pliable.*

Steak Diane with Cremini Mushrooms

Makes 2 servings

4 teaspoons olive oil, divided

2 beef tenderloin steaks
   (4 ounces each), cut
   ¾ inch thick

¼ teaspoon black pepper

⅓ cup sliced shallots or
   chopped onion

4 ounces cremini
   mushrooms, sliced *or*
   1 (4-ounce) package
   sliced mixed wild
   mushrooms

1½ tablespoons
   Worcestershire sauce

1 tablespoon Dijon mustard

1. Heat 2 teaspoons oil in large skillet over medium-high heat. Add steaks; sprinkle with pepper. Cook 3 minutes per side for medium rare or to desired doneness. Remove to plate; tent with foil to keep warm.

2. Add remaining 2 teaspoons oil to skillet; heat over medium heat. Add shallots; cook and stir 2 minutes. Add mushrooms; cook and stir 3 minutes. Add Worcestershire sauce and mustard; cook 1 minute, stirring frequently.

3. Return steaks and any accumulated juices to skillet; heat through, turning once. Transfer steaks to serving plates; top with mushroom mixture.

2 teaspoons vegetable oil,
   divided

1 package (6 ounces)
   fresh spinach,
   stemmed and torn

8 ounces boneless beef top
   sirloin steak, thinly sliced

¼ cup stir-fry sauce

1 teaspoon sugar

½ teaspoon curry powder

¼ teaspoon ground ginger

Stir-Fried Beef and Spinach

Makes 2 servings

1. Heat 1 teaspoon oil in large skillet or wok over high heat. Add spinach; stir-fry 1 minute or until wilted. Remove to serving platter or plate; keep warm.

2. Add remaining 1 teaspoon oil to skillet; heat over high heat. Add beef; stir-fry 2 minutes or until barely pink.

3. Add stir-fry sauce, sugar, curry powder and ginger to skillet; cook and stir 1 to 2 minutes or until sauce thickens. Serve over spinach.

Orange Teriyaki Pork Packets

Makes 2 servings

8 ounces pork stew meat (1-inch pieces)

1½ cups frozen bell pepper blend for stir-fry

¼ cup water chestnuts, coarsely chopped

2 sheets (18×12 inches each) heavy-duty foil, lightly sprayed with nonstick cooking spray

1 tablespoon cornstarch

2 tablespoons teriyaki sauce

2 tablespoons orange marmalade

½ teaspoon dry mustard

¼ teaspoon ground ginger

Hot cooked rice

1. Preheat oven to 450°F.

2. Combine pork, bell peppers and water chestnuts in medium bowl; toss to mix. Place half of mixture on each foil sheet.

3. Dissolve cornstarch in teriyaki sauce in small bowl. Stir in marmalade, mustard and ginger. Pour mixture over pork and vegetables.

4. Double fold sides and ends of foil to seal packets, leaving head space for heat circulation. Place packets on baking sheet.

5. Bake 20 to 23 minutes or until pork is tender. Remove from oven. Carefully open one end of each packet to allow steam to escape. Open packets and transfer contents to serving plates. Serve with rice.

Beef & Pork

6 tablespoons wasabi
    horseradish

2 tablespoons olive oil

1 beef flank steak
    (1 to 1½ pounds)

2 large red potatoes, cut
    into ¼-inch-thick slices

¼ cup water

1 teaspoon salt

Grilled Wasabi Flank Steak

Makes 2 servings

1. Combine horseradish and oil in small bowl; mix well. Spread 2 tablespoons mixture on both sides of steak. Marinate in refrigerator 30 minutes or up to 2 hours.

2. Combine potatoes, water and salt in medium microwavable dish; cover and microwave on HIGH 5 minutes. Drain potatoes. Add 2 tablespoons horseradish mixture; toss to coat.

3. Prepare grill for direct cooking.

4. Grill steak, covered, over medium heat 8 minutes; turn. Place potatoes on grid. Brush potatoes; then steak with remaining horseradish mixture. Grill 8 to 10 minutes or until steak is medium rare (145°F) and potatoes are lightly browned. Season with salt.

4 cups water

1 large russet potato (about 8 ounces), peeled and quartered

¼ cup milk, heated

1 tablespoon butter

½ teaspoon salt, divided

Dash white pepper

2 teaspoons olive oil

2 tablespoons chopped onion

1 clove garlic, minced

1 cup chopped mushrooms

8 ounces ground beef

1 tablespoon all-purpose flour

1 cup beef broth

2 small carrots, diced

2 small parsnips, diced

1 teaspoon dried parsley flakes

⅛ teaspoon black pepper

½ cup frozen peas

¼ cup chopped leeks

Individual Shepherd's Pie

Makes 2 servings

1. Preheat oven to 400°F.

2. Bring water to a boil in medium saucepan over high heat. Add potato; cook 15 to 18 minutes or until tender. Drain and return potato to saucepan; shake over low heat to dry up remaining water on potato. Mash potato with potato masher. Add milk, butter, ¼ teaspoon salt and white pepper; mash until smooth. Set aside.

3. Heat oil in medium skillet over medium heat. Add onion and garlic; cook and stir about 2 minutes or until softened. Add mushrooms; cook about 5 minutes or until mushrooms lose their moisture and begin to brown, stirring occasionally Transfer vegetables to bowl.

4. Cook beef in same skillet over medium heat 6 to 8 minutes or until browned, stirring to break up meat. Drain fat. Add mushroom mixture and flour; cook and stir 3 minutes. Add broth, carrots, parsnips, parsley flakes, remaining ¼ teaspoon salt and black pepper; bring to a boil. Reduce heat to low; cook until thickened, stirring frequently. Add peas and leeks; cook until tender.

5. Spoon mixture into two 10-ounce ramekins or small casseroles. Spread mashed potatoes on top of each serving. Place ramekins on baking sheet.

6. Bake 20 minutes or until heated through.

Beef & Pork

Balsamic Grilled Pork Chops

Makes 2 servings

2 tablespoons balsamic vinegar

2 tablespoons soy sauce

1 teaspoon Dijon mustard

2 teaspoons sugar

⅛ teaspoon red pepper flakes

2 boneless pork chops, trimmed (about 4 ounces each)

1. Combine vinegar, soy sauce, mustard, sugar and red pepper flakes in small bowl; mix well. Reserve 1 tablespoon marinade for serving.

2. Place pork in large resealable food storage bag. Pour remaining marinade over pork. Seal bag; turn to coat. Refrigerate 2 hours or up to 24 hours.

3. Spray grill pan with nonstick cooking spray; heat over medium-high heat. Remove pork from marinade; discard marinade.

4. Cook pork about 4 minutes per side or just until slightly pink in center. Drizzle with reserved 1 tablespoon marinade.

6 ounces ground beef

½ cup chopped green
  bell pepper

½ teaspoon ground cumin

½ teaspoon chili powder

⅛ teaspoon ground
  cinnamon

½ cup chunky salsa

1 tablespoon golden raisins

4 (6-inch) white corn or
  flour tortillas, warmed

½ cup shredded lettuce

¼ cup (1 ounce) shredded
  Cheddar cheese

1 small tomato, chopped

Picadillo Tacos

Makes 2 servings

1. Combine beef, bell pepper, cumin, chili powder and cinnamon in large skillet; cook over medium heat 6 to 8 minutes or until meat is browned, stirring to break up meat. Drain fat.

2. Add salsa and raisins; cook over low heat 5 minutes, stirring occasionally.

3. Divide meat mixture evenly among tortillas. Top with lettuce, cheese and tomato.

Meatless Meals

Roasted Chickpea and Sweet Potato Bowl

Makes 2 servings

- 1 sweet potato (about 12 ounces)
- 1 tablespoon plus 1 teaspoon olive oil, divided
- 1 teaspoon salt, divided
  Black pepper
- 1 can (about 15 ounces) chickpeas, rinsed and drained
- 1 tablespoon maple syrup
- 1 teaspoon paprika, sweet or smoked
- ½ teaspoon ground cumin
- ½ cup uncooked quinoa
- 1 cup water
  Chopped fresh parsley or cilantro

Tahini Sauce

- ¼ cup tahini
- 2 tablespoons lemon juice
- 2 tablespoons water
- 1 clove garlic, minced
- ⅛ teaspoon salt

1. Preheat oven to 350°F.

2. Peel sweet potato; cut in half crosswise. Spiral sweet potato with thin ribbon blade of spiralizer. Cut into 3-inch pieces. Place in 13×9-inch baking pan. Drizzle with 1 teaspoon oil and sprinkle with ¼ teaspoon salt and black pepper; toss to coat. Push to one side of pan.

3. Combine chickpeas, maple syrup, remaining 1 tablespoon oil, paprika, cumin and ½ teaspoon salt in medium bowl; toss to coat. Spread in other side of pan. Roast 30 minutes, stirring sweet potatoes and chickpeas once or twice.

4. Meanwhile, place quinoa in fine-mesh strainer; rinse well under cold water. Bring 1 cup water, quinoa and remaining ¼ teaspoon salt to a boil in small saucepan over high heat. Reduce heat to low; cover and simmer 10 to 15 minutes or until quinoa is tender and water is absorbed.

5. For sauce, whisk tahini, lemon juice, 2 tablespoons water, garlic and ⅛ teaspoon salt in small bowl until smooth. Add additional water if needed to reach desired consistency.

6. Divide quinoa between two bowls; top with sweet potatoes and chickpeas. Sprinkle with parsley; serve with sauce.

Note: If you don't have a spiralizer, julienne the sweet potato or cut it into cubes instead.

2 tablespoons extra virgin
olive oil

4 slices Italian bread

2 ounces fresh mozzarella
cheese, cut into slices
or ½ cup shredded
mozzarella cheese

2 plum tomatoes, sliced

4 fresh basil leaves

8 pitted kalamata olives,
cut in half

Waffled Caprese Panini

Makes 2 servings

1. Preheat waffle maker to medium.

2. Brush oil on both sides of bread slices. Top two slices bread with cheese, tomatoes, basil, olives and remaining bread slices.

3. Place sandwiches, one at a time, in waffle maker; close while pressing down slightly. Cook 2 minutes or until bread is golden brown and cheese is melted.

Peanut Noodles

Makes 2 servings

1½ tablespoons vegetable oil, divided

1 tablespoon lime juice

1 tablespoon peanut butter

½ tablespoon teriyaki sauce

½ teaspoon chili-garlic paste (optional)

1 package (3 ounces) ramen noodles*

⅓ cup shelled edamame, thawed if frozen

¼ cup thinly sliced red bell pepper

Crushed peanuts (optional)

Use any flavor; discard seasoning packets.

1. Whisk 1 tablespoon oil, lime juice, peanut butter, teriyaki sauce and chili-garlic paste, if desired, in large bowl until well blended.

2. Bring water to a boil in large saucepan over medium-high heat. Add noodles and edamame; boil 2 minutes. Rinse and drain under cold water. Toss with remaining ½ tablespoon oil.

3. Add noodle mixture and bell pepper to peanut butter mixture; toss to coat. Top with peanuts, if desired.

Meatless Meals

- ½ teaspoon salt
- ½ teaspoon smoked paprika
- ½ teaspoon onion powder
- ¼ teaspoon garlic powder
- ¼ teaspoon ground cumin
- ¼ teaspoon black pepper
- 2 portobello mushroom caps
- 1 tablespoon plus 1 teaspoon olive oil, divided
- ½ small yellow onion, finely chopped
- 2 tablespoons ketchup
- 1 tablespoon apple cider vinegar
- ½ tablespoon Dijon mustard
- ½ tablespoon packed brown sugar
- ½ teaspoon soy sauce
- 2 hamburger buns
- Mayonnaise, sliced dill pickles and/or shredded cabbage or lettuce

BBQ Portobellos

Makes 2 servings

1. Preheat oven to 375°F. Line baking sheet with parchment paper.

2. Combine salt, paprika, onion powder, garlic powder, cumin and pepper in small bowl; mix well. Scrape gills from mushrooms and remove any stem. Cut mushrooms into ½-inch slices; place in large bowl. Drizzle with 1 tablespoon oil; toss to coat. Add seasoning mixture; toss until well blended. Arrange mushroom slices in single layer on prepared baking sheet.

3. Bake 15 minutes. Turn and bake 5 minutes or until mushrooms are tender and have shrunk slightly.

4. Meanwhile, heat remaining 1 teaspoon oil in small saucepan over medium-high heat. Add onion; cook and stir 5 minutes or until onion is very soft. Add ketchup, vinegar, mustard, brown sugar and soy sauce; mix well. Reduce heat to low; cook 5 minutes, stirring occasionally.

5. Combine mushrooms and sauce in large bowl; stir to coat. Serve on buns with mayonnaise, pickles and cabbage.

Note: For a smoother sauce, process in a mini food processor or blender until smooth.

Meatless Meals

½ cup chopped seeded
tomato

¼ cup chunky salsa

¼ cup frozen corn, thawed

¼ cup canned black beans,
rinsed and drained

1 teaspoon chopped
fresh cilantro

¼ teaspoon chopped garlic

Dash ground red pepper

1 cup cooked brown rice

Shredded Cheddar cheese
(optional)

South-of-the-Border Lunch Express

Makes 2 servings

1. Combine tomato, salsa, corn, beans, cilantro, garlic and red pepper in medium microwavable bowl. Cover with vented plastic wrap; microwave on HIGH 1 to 1½ minutes or until heated through, stirring after 1 minute.

2. Microwave rice in small microwavable bowl on HIGH 1 to 1½ minutes or until heated through. Top with tomato mixture and cheese, if desired.

Variation: To make this vegetarian dish even more hearty and satisfying, add ½ cup pinto beans.

4 ounces uncooked whole
    grain penne pasta

1 can (about 15 ounces) navy
    beans, rinsed and drained

1 tablespoon olive oil

1 cup diced green
    bell pepper

½ cup grape tomatoes,
    halved

2 tablespoons chopped
    fresh basil

¼ teaspoon salt

2 ounces crumbled
    feta cheese

Italian Garden Penne

Makes 2 servings

1. Cook pasta according to package directions; add beans during last minute of cooking.

2. Meanwhile heat oil in large skillet over medium-high heat. Add bell pepper; cook 4 minutes or until crisp-tender, stirring frequently. Add tomatoes; cook 4 minutes or until tender, stirring occasionally. Remove from heat.

3. Drain pasta and beans; place in shallow serving bowl. Sprinkle with basil and salt; top with pepper mixture and cheese.

Khachapuri (Georgian Cheese Bread)

Makes 2 servings

1 loaf (16 ounces) frozen bread dough, thawed according to package directions

1½ cups (6 ounces) shredded mozzarella cheese

1½ cups (6 ounces) crumbled feta cheese

1 teaspoon olive oil

1 teaspoon everything bagel seasoning (optional)

2 eggs

Black pepper

1. Line baking sheet with parchment paper. Divide dough in half. Roll out one half into 11×8½-inch oval on lightly floured surface. Transfer to prepared baking sheet.

2. Combine mozzarella and feta in medium bowl; mix well. Sprinkle ½ cup cheese mixture over dough, spreading almost to edges. Starting with long sides of oval, roll up dough and cheese towards center, curving into boat shape and leaving about 3 inches open in center. Press ends to seal. Fill center with 1 cup cheese mixture. Repeat rolling and filling steps with remaining half of dough and cheese mixture.

3. Cover loosely with plastic wrap; let rise 20 to 30 minutes or until puffy. Preheat oven to 400°F. Just before baking, brush edges of dough with oil; sprinkle with everything bagel seasoning, if desired.

4. Bake 12 minutes. Remove baking sheet from oven; use back of spoon to create indentations for eggs in center of cheese. Crack egg into each indentation;* sprinkle with pepper.

5. Bake 8 minutes for soft eggs; bake 1 to 2 minutes longer for firmer eggs.

For more control, crack egg into small bowl and slide egg from bowl into cheese mixture.

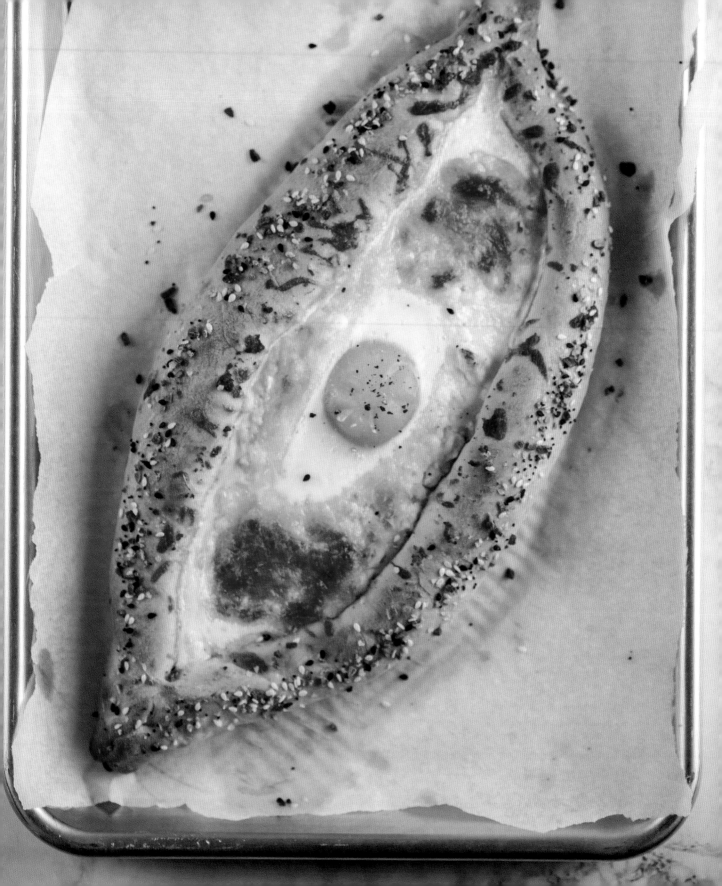

1 package (14 ounces) firm tofu, drained

¼ cup soy sauce

1 tablespoon creamy peanut butter

1 medium zucchini

1 medium yellow squash

1 medium red bell pepper

2 teaspoons peanut or vegetable oil

½ teaspoon hot chili oil

2 cloves garlic, minced

2 cups packed torn stemmed fresh spinach

Hot cooked rice (optional)

¼ cup coarsely chopped cashew nuts or peanuts

Dragon Tofu

Makes 2 servings

1. Press tofu lightly between paper towels; cut into ¾-inch triangles or squares. Place in single layer in shallow dish.

2. Whisk soy sauce into peanut butter in small bowl until smooth. Pour mixture over tofu; stir gently to coat. Let stand at room temperature 20 minutes.

3. Meanwhile, cut zucchini and yellow squash lengthwise into ¼-inch-thick slices; cut each slice into 2-inch strips. Cut bell pepper into 2-inch strips.

4. Heat peanut oil and chili oil in large skillet or wok over medium-high heat. Add garlic, zucchini, yellow squash and bell pepper; stir-fry 3 minutes. Add tofu mixture; cook 2 minutes or until tofu is heated through and sauce is slightly thickened, stirring occasionally.

5. Stir in spinach; remove from heat. Serve with rice, if desired; sprinkle with cashews.

Hummus Pita Pizzas

Makes 2 servings

½ (15-ounce) can chickpeas, drained

1½ tablespoons olive oil

1 teaspoon lemon juice

½ teaspoon minced garlic

¼ teaspoon salt

⅛ teaspoon ground red pepper

2 pita bread rounds

½ cup chopped tomato

¼ cup black olives, drained

¾ cup (3 ounces) shredded mozzarella cheese

1. Preheat oven to 425°F. Combine chickpeas, oil, lemon juice, garlic, salt and red pepper in food processor or blender; process until smooth.

2. Spread bean mixture over pita breads; top with tomato, olives and cheese. Place on baking sheet.

3. Bake 8 to 10 minutes or until cheese is melted and pizzas are heated through.

Creamy Fettuccine with Asparagus and Lima Beans

Makes 2 servings

- 4 ounces uncooked fettuccine
- 1 tablespoon butter
- 1 cup fresh asparagus pieces (about 1 inch)
- ½ cup frozen lima beans, thawed
- ½ teaspoon salt
- ¼ teaspoon black pepper
- ¼ cup vegetable broth
- ½ cup half-and-half or whipping cream
- ½ cup grated Parmesan cheese

1. Cook fettuccine according to package directions. Drain well; cover and keep warm.

2. Meanwhile, melt butter in large skillet over medium-high heat. Add asparagus, lima beans, salt and pepper; cook and stir 3 minutes. Add broth; cook 3 minutes. Add half-and-half; cook 3 to 4 minutes or until vegetables are tender.

3. Add fettuccine and cheese to skillet; stir to blend. Serve immediately.

Tuscan Portobello Melt

Makes 2 servings

- 1 portobello mushroom cap, thinly sliced
- ½ small red onion, thinly sliced
- ½ cup grape tomatoes
- 1 tablespoon olive oil
- 1 teaspoon balsamic vinegar
- ⅛ teaspoon salt
- ⅛ teaspoon dried thyme
- ⅛ teaspoon black pepper
- 2 tablespoons butter, softened and divided
- 4 slices sourdough bread
- 2 slices (about 1 ounce each) provolone cheese
- 2 teaspoons Dijon mustard
- 2 slices (1 ounce each) Monterey Jack cheese

1. Preheat broiler. Combine mushroom, onion and tomatoes in small baking pan. Drizzle with oil and vinegar; sprinkle with salt, thyme and pepper. Toss to coat. Spread vegetables in single layer in pan.

2. Broil 6 minutes or until vegetables are softened and browned, stirring once.

3. Heat medium skillet over medium heat. Spread 1 tablespoon butter over one side of each bread slice. Place buttered side down in skillet; cook 2 minutes or until bread is toasted. Transfer bread to cutting board, toasted sides up.

4. Place provolone on two bread slices; spread mustard over cheese. Top with vegetables, Monterey Jack and remaining bread slices, toasted sides down. Spread remaining 1 tablespoon butter on outside of sandwiches. Cook in same skillet over medium heat 5 minutes or until bread is toasted and cheese is melted, turning once.

Quinoa Burrito Bowls

Makes 2 servings

½ cup uncooked quinoa

1 cup water

1 tablespoon lime juice, divided

2 teaspoons olive oil

1 small onion, diced

½ red bell pepper, diced

½ teaspoon minced garlic

¼ cup thawed frozen corn

¼ cup canned black beans, rinsed and drained

2 tablespoons sour cream

   Shredded lettuce

   Lime wedges

1. Place quinoa in fine-mesh strainer; rinse well under cold water. Bring 1 cup water and quinoa to a boil in small saucepan over high heat. Reduce heat to low; cover and cook 10 to 15 minutes or until quinoa is tender and water is absorbed. Stir in half of lime juice; cover and keep warm.

2. Meanwhile, heat oil in large skillet over medium heat. Add onion and bell pepper; cook and stir 5 minutes or until softened. Add garlic; cook and stir 1 minute. Add corn and beans; cook 3 to 5 minutes or until heated through.

3. Combine sour cream and remaining lime juice in small bowl; mix well.

4. Divide quinoa among two serving bowls; top with vegetable mixture, lettuce and sour cream mixture. Serve with lime wedges.

Meatless Meals

1 tablespoon olive oil

1 cup thinly sliced onion

1 cup chopped green bell pepper

1 clove garlic, minced

1 tablespoon ketchup

½ tablespoon yellow mustard

½ (15-ounce) can kidney beans, rinsed, drained and mashed

½ cup tomato sauce

½ teaspoon chili powder

¼ teaspoon salt

2 teaspoons cider vinegar

2 sandwich rolls, split

Meatless Sloppy Joes

Makes 2 servings

1. Heat oil in large skillet over medium heat. Add onion, bell pepper and garlic; cook and stir about 5 minutes or until vegetables are tender. Stir in ketchup and mustard.

2. Stir in beans, tomato sauce, chili powder and salt; mix well. Reduce heat to medium-low; cook 5 minutes or until thickened, stirring frequently. Stir in vinegar. Serve on rolls.

Savory Sides

Savory Sides

Artichokes with Lemon-Tarragon Butter

Makes 2 servings

6 cups water

2¼ teaspoons salt, divided

2 whole artichokes, stems cut off and leaf tips trimmed

¼ cup (½ stick) butter

2 tablespoons lemon juice

¼ teaspoon grated lemon peel

¼ teaspoon dried tarragon

1. Combine water and 2 teaspoons salt in large saucepan; bring to a boil over high heat. Add artichokes; return to a boil. Reduce heat to medium-low; cover and simmer 35 to 45 minutes or until artichoke leaves detach easily.

2. Turn artichokes upside down to drain well. Cut artichokes in half vertically; use spoon to remove fuzzy chokes near stem.

3. Combine butter, lemon juice, lemon peel, tarragon and remaining ¼ teaspoon salt in small saucepan; heat over low heat until butter is melted. Serve in small bowls for dipping.

Savory Sides

1 carrot, quartered
  lengthwise and cut
  into 2-inch pieces

1 medium sweet potato,
  peeled and cut into
  ¾-inch pieces

½ red bell pepper, cut
  into 1-inch pieces

½ medium onion, cut
  into ½-inch wedges

1 tablespoon dark
  sesame oil, divided

2 teaspoons sugar, divided

¼ teaspoon salt

1 teaspoon rice vinegar
  or lime juice

Rich Roasted
Sesame Vegetables

Makes 2 servings

1. Preheat oven to 425°F. Line large baking sheet
with foil.

2. Combine carrot, sweet potato, bell pepper and onion
on prepared baking sheet; drizzle with 2 teaspoons oil.
Sprinkle with 1 teaspoon sugar and salt; toss gently to
coat. Arrange vegetables in single layer.

3. Roast 20 minutes or until edges of vegetables are
browned and sweet potato is tender when pierced with
fork, stirring once halfway through cooking time. Add
remaining 1 teaspoon oil, 1 teaspoon sugar and vinegar;
toss gently to coat.

Savory Sides

3 tablespoons olive oil, divided

1 medium spaghetti squash (2 to 2½ pounds)

¼ teaspoon plus ⅛ teaspoon salt, divided

1 clove garlic, minced

¼ teaspoon red pepper flakes

⅛ teaspoon black pepper

½ cup shredded Parmesan cheese

⅓ cup chopped fresh parsley

Garlic Parmesan Spaghetti Squash

Makes 2 servings

1. Preheat oven to 400°F. Brush baking sheet with 1 teaspoon oil. Cut squash in half; remove and discard seeds. Brush each cut side with 1 teaspoon oil and sprinkle with ⅛ teaspoon salt. Place squash cut sides down on prepared baking sheet.

2. Bake 30 to 40 minutes or until squash is fork-tender.

3. Remove squash to plate; let stand until cool enough to handle. Use fork to shred squash into long strands, reserving shells for serving, if desired.

4. Heat remaining 2 tablespoons oil in large nonstick skillet over medium-high heat. Add garlic, remaining ⅛ teaspoon salt, red pepper flakes and black pepper; cook and stir 2 to 3 minutes or until garlic begins to turn golden. Turn off heat. Add squash, cheese and parsley to skillet; stir gently just until blended. Serve immediately.

Asparagus with Lemon and Mustard

Makes 2 servings

12 fresh asparagus spears

2 tablespoons mayonnaise

1 tablespoon spicy
   brown mustard

1 tablespoon lemon juice

⅛ teaspoon salt

1 teaspoon grated lemon
   peel, divided

1. Fill large saucepan with 1 inch water; bring to a boil over high heat. Place asparagus in steamer basket; steam until crisp-tender. Rinse under cold water; drain and chill.

2. Whisk mayonnaise, mustard, lemon juice and salt in small bowl until well blended. Stir in ½ teaspoon lemon peel.

3. Divide asparagus between two plates; spoon 2 tablespoons dressing over each serving. Top with remaining ½ teaspoon lemon peel.

Sweet Potato Noodles with Blue Cheese and Walnuts

Makes 2 servings

2 sweet potatoes
  (1½ pounds)

¼ cup chopped walnuts

1 tablespoon olive oil

2 cloves garlic, minced

¼ cup whipping cream

1 package (5 ounces)
  baby spinach

¼ teaspoon salt

¼ teaspoon black pepper

¼ cup crumbled blue cheese

1. Spiral sweet potatoes with thin ribbon blade. Loosely pile on cutting board and cut in an X.

2. Cook walnuts in large nonstick skillet over medium-high heat 3 to 4 minutes or until toasted, stirring frequently. Remove to plate; cool completely.

3. Heat oil in same skillet over medium-high heat. Add sweet potatoes; cook and stir 10 minutes or until sweet potatoes reach desired doneness, adding water by tablespoonfuls if browning too quickly.

4. Add garlic to skillet; cook and stir 30 seconds. Add cream and spinach; cook and stir 1 minute or until cream is absorbed and spinach is wilted. Season with salt and pepper. Transfer to serving bowls; top with walnuts and cheese.

1 tablespoon minced fresh dill, thyme or rosemary leaves *or* 1 teaspoon dried dill weed, thyme or rosemary

⅛ teaspoon garlic salt

Pinch black pepper

2 peeled medium red potatoes (about ¼ pound)

2 teaspoons olive oil

Sour cream

Herbed Potato Chips

Makes 2 servings

1. Preheat oven to 450°F. Spray baking sheets with nonstick cooking spray. Combine dill, garlic salt and pepper in small bowl; mix well.

2. Cut potatoes crosswise into very thin slices (about 1/16 inch thick). Pat dry with paper towels. Arrange potato slices in single layer on prepared baking sheets; spray with cooking spray.

3. Bake 10 minutes; turn potatoes. Brush with oil; sprinkle evenly with seasoning mixture.

4. Bake 5 to 10 minutes or until golden brown. Cool on baking sheets. Serve with sour cream.

Zucchini Ribbon Salad

Makes 2 servings

2 medium zucchini

2 tablespoons chopped
   sun-dried tomatoes
   (not packed in oil)

1 tablespoon olive oil

1 teaspoon lemon juice

1 teaspoon white vinegar

¼ teaspoon salt

2 tablespoons shredded
   Parmesan cheese

1 tablespoon pine nuts,
   toasted*

**To toast pine nuts, cook in
small skillet over medium heat
1 to 2 minutes or until lightly
browned, stirring frequently.*

1. Cut zucchini into ribbons with vegetable peeler. Combine zucchini and sun-dried tomatoes in medium bowl.

2. Whisk oil, lemon juice, vinegar and salt in small bowl until well blended. Drizzle over zucchini and tomatoes; toss gently to coat.

3. Divide salad between two serving bowls; top with cheese and pine nuts. Serve immediately.

Vegetable Couscous

Makes 2 servings

- ½ small bulb fennel
- 1 tablespoon olive oil
- ⅓ cup thinly sliced carrots
- ¼ cup chopped shallots or onion
- 1 clove garlic, minced
- ⅓ cup water
- ⅓ cup vegetable juice cocktail
- ⅛ teaspoon salt
- ¼ teaspoon hot pepper sauce
- ⅓ cup whole wheat or regular couscous

1. Chop and reserve 1 tablespoon fennel fronds for garnish. Trim and chop fennel bulb. (You should have about ½ cup.)

2. Heat oil in medium saucepan over medium heat. Add chopped fennel bulb, carrots, shallots and garlic; cook 5 minutes, stirring occasionally. Add water, vegetable juice, salt and hot pepper sauce; bring to a simmer. Reduce heat to medium-low; cover and cook 5 to 6 minutes or until vegetables are tender.

3. Stir in couscous. Turn off heat, cover and let stand 5 minutes or until liquid is absorbed.

4. Stir couscous with fork; garnish with reserved fennel fronds.

Sweet Potato Fries

Makes 2 servings

1 large sweet potato
   (about 8 ounces)

1 tablespoon olive oil

¼ teaspoon coarse salt

¼ teaspoon black pepper

¼ teaspoon ground
   red pepper

   Honey or maple syrup
   (optional)

1. Preheat oven to 425°F. Spray baking sheet with nonstick cooking spray.

2. Peel sweet potato; cut lengthwise into long spears. Toss with oil, salt, black pepper and red pepper on prepared baking sheet. Spread sweet potato in single layer not touching.

3. Bake 20 to 30 minutes or until lightly browned, turning halfway through cooking time. Serve with honey, if desired.

Savory Sides

1 tablespoon butter

2 small carrots, diagonally cut into thin slices

1 clove garlic, minced

½ teaspoon dried basil, dill weed or tarragon

1 small red bell pepper, cut into thin strips

1 medium yellow squash, cut into matchsticks

4 jarred artichoke hearts, drained and rinsed, cut into quarters

1½ teaspoons lemon juice

Salt and black pepper

Carrot-Artichoke Sauté

Makes 2 servings

1. Melt butter in large skillet over medium heat. Add carrots, garlic and basil; cook and stir 2 minutes. Add bell pepper; cook and stir 2 minutes. Add yellow squash and artichokes; cook and stir 3 minutes.

2. Stir in lemon juice; cook 1 minute. Season with salt and black pepper.

Sweet Treats

Sweet 'n' Easy
Fruit Crisp Bowls

Makes 2 servings

2 tablespoons granola
   with almonds

1 tablespoon butter

1 red apple (8 ounces),
   such as Gala, cut
   into ½-inch pieces

1 tablespoon dried
   sweetened cranberries

¼ teaspoon apple pie spice
   or ground cinnamon

2 teaspoons sugar

¼ teaspoon almond extract

   Vanilla ice cream

1. Place granola in small resealable food storage bag; crush lightly to form coarse crumbs. Set aside.

2. Melt butter in large skillet over medium heat. Add apple, cranberries and apple pie spice; cook 4 minutes or just until apple is tender, stirring frequently.

3. Remove from heat, stir in sugar and almond extract. Spoon into two dessert bowls or dessert plates. Sprinkle with granola; top with ice cream. Serve immediately.

Note: *The apple mixture can be made up to 8 hours in advance; top with granola and ice cream when ready to serve. To reheat the crisp, microwave the apple mixture on HIGH 20 to 30 seconds or just until warm.*

Individual Chocolate Soufflés

Makes 2 servings

1 teaspoon butter, divided

5 tablespoons granulated sugar, divided

4 ounces semisweet chocolate, chopped

2 ounces cream cheese, softened

2 tablespoons milk

2 eggs, separated, at room temperature

Pinch salt

Powdered sugar

1. Use ½ teaspoon butter to grease two 10-ounce custard cups. Add 1 tablespoon granulated sugar; shake to coat bottoms and sides of cups.

2. To make collars for cups, fold 16-inch-long piece of foil in half lengthwise, then fold in half again. Use ¼ teaspoon butter to grease half of foil lengthwise. Sprinkle buttered half with 1½ teaspoons granulated sugar. Wrap foil around custard cup, buttered side in; allow buttered half to extend 1 inch above rim. If necessary, secure with masking tape. Repeat for second collar.

3. Preheat oven to 350°F. Place small baking pan in oven. Combine chocolate, cream cheese and milk in microwavable bowl; microwave on HIGH 1 minute. Stir until smooth. If mixture is not completely melted, microwave at 30-second intervals, stirring after each interval. Cool slightly, then stir in egg yolks until well blended.

4. Beat egg whites in medium bowl with electric mixer at high speed until frothy. Add salt, then gradually add remaining 3 tablespoons granulated sugar, beating until stiff peaks form. Gently fold chocolate mixture into egg whites in three additions. Divide batter between custard cups; place cups in preheated baking pan.

5. Bake 35 to 40 minutes or until soufflés are puffed and toothpick inserted into centers comes out clean. Remove collars; sprinkle with powdered sugar. Serve immediately (soufflés deflate as they cool).

Sweet Treats

Broiled Pineapple with Spiced Vanilla Sauce

Makes 2 servings

3 ounces cream cheese, softened

¼ cup granulated sugar

¼ cup evaporated milk or half-and-half

¼ teaspoon pumpkin pie spice or Chinese five-spice powder

¼ teaspoon vanilla

1 sheet (14×12 inches) heavy-duty foil

2 teaspoons butter, softened

4 thick slices fresh pineapple, skin and eyes trimmed

2 tablespoons packed brown sugar

1. Preheat broiler. Whisk cream cheese, granulated sugar, evaporated milk, pumpkin pie spice and vanilla in medium bowl until smooth. Refrigerate until ready to serve.

2. Coat center of foil sheet with butter. Place pineapple slices side by side on foil; sprinkle with brown sugar. Fold up sides and ends of foil around pineapple, leaving top open. Place on baking sheet.

3. Broil pineapple 4 inches from heat 10 to 12 minutes or until surface of pineapple is bubbling and lightly browned. Watch pineapple closely during last 5 minutes to avoid burning.

4. Spoon cream cheese mixture on serving plates; top with pineapple.

Pumpkin Bread Pudding

Makes 2 servings

2   slices whole wheat bread

1   cup canned pumpkin

1   egg

2   tablespoons sugar

1   teaspoon vanilla

½   teaspoon ground
    cinnamon, plus additional
    for garnish

⅛   teaspoon salt

1   tablespoon raisins

    Whipped topping
    (optional)

1. Preheat oven to 375°F. Spray two ovenproof custard cups or ramekins with nonstick cooking spray. Toast bread; cut into 1-inch cubes.

2. Whisk pumpkin, egg, sugar, vanilla, ½ teaspoon cinnamon and salt in medium bowl until well blended. Fold in toasted bread cubes and raisins. Divide evenly between prepared cups.

3. Bake 30 minutes. Serve warm with whipped topping, if desired. Garnish with additional cinnamon.

½ cup peeled fresh peach
or nectarine chunks
(½-inch pieces)

1 can (5 ounces)
evaporated milk*

1 egg

1 teaspoon sugar

½ teaspoon vanilla

Ground cinnamon
(optional)

*If a 5-ounce can is not available,
use ½ cup plus 2 tablespoons
evaporated milk.

Peach Custard

Makes 2 servings

1. Preheat oven to 325°F. Divide peaches between two 6-ounce ovenproof custard cups.

2. Whisk evaporated milk, egg, sugar and vanilla in small bowl until well blended. Pour mixture over peaches.

3. Place custard cups in shallow 1-quart baking pan. Carefully pour hot water into pan to depth of 1 inch.

4. Bake 50 minutes or until knife inserted into centers comes out clean. Remove custard cups from water bath; serve warm or at room temperature. Sprinkle with cinnamon, if desired, just before serving.

Note: Drained canned peach slices in juice can be substituted for fresh fruit.

4 whole ladyfingers, broken
    into bite-size pieces

6 tablespoons cold strong
    coffee *or* ½ teaspoon
    instant coffee granules
    dissolved in ⅓ cup water

2 teaspoons sugar

½ teaspoon vanilla

½ cup thawed frozen
    whipped topping

1½ teaspoons unsweetened
    cocoa powder

1 tablespoon sliced almonds

Tiramisù Cups

Makes 2 servings

1. Divide ladyfinger pieces between two 6-ounce custard cups.

2. Combine coffee, sugar and vanilla in small bowl; stir until sugar is dissolved. Drizzle half of coffee mixture over each serving.

3. Place whipped topping in small bowl; gently fold in cocoa. Spoon mixture over ladyfingers. Cover with plastic wrap; refrigerate at least 2 hours.

4. Toast almonds in small skillet over medium-high heat 2 to 3 minutes or until golden brown, stirring constantly. Transfer to small bowl; cool completely. Sprinkle over desserts just before serving.

Index

188

Metric Conversion Chart

VOLUME MEASUREMENTS (dry)

$1/8$ teaspoon = 0.5 mL
$1/4$ teaspoon = 1 mL
$1/2$ teaspoon = 2 mL
$3/4$ teaspoon = 4 mL
1 teaspoon = 5 mL
1 tablespoon = 15 mL
2 tablespoons = 30 mL
$1/4$ cup = 60 mL
$1/3$ cup = 75 mL
$1/2$ cup = 125 mL
$2/3$ cup = 150 mL
$3/4$ cup = 175 mL
1 cup = 250 mL
2 cups = 1 pint = 500 mL
3 cups = 750 mL
4 cups = 1 quart = 1 L

VOLUME MEASUREMENTS (fluid)

1 fluid ounce (2 tablespoons) = 30 mL
4 fluid ounces ($1/2$ cup) = 125 mL
8 fluid ounces (1 cup) = 250 mL
12 fluid ounces ($1 1/2$ cups) = 375 mL
16 fluid ounces (2 cups) = 500 mL

WEIGHTS (mass)

$1/2$ ounce = 15 g
1 ounce = 30 g
3 ounces = 90 g
4 ounces = 120 g
8 ounces = 225 g
10 ounces = 285 g
12 ounces = 360 g
16 ounces = 1 pound = 450 g

DIMENSIONS

$1/16$ inch = 2 mm
$1/8$ inch = 3 mm
$1/4$ inch = 6 mm
$1/2$ inch = 1.5 cm
$3/4$ inch = 2 cm
1 inch = 2.5 cm

OVEN TEMPERATURES

250°F = 120°C
275°F = 140°C
300°F = 150°C
325°F = 160°C
350°F = 180°C
375°F = 190°C
400°F = 200°C
425°F = 220°C
450°F = 230°C

BAKING PAN SIZES

Utensil	Size in Inches/Quarts	Metric Volume	Size in Centimeters
Baking or Cake Pan (square or rectangular)	$8 \times 8 \times 2$	2 L	$20 \times 20 \times 5$
	$9 \times 9 \times 2$	2.5 L	$23 \times 23 \times 5$
	$12 \times 8 \times 2$	3 L	$30 \times 20 \times 5$
	$13 \times 9 \times 2$	3.5 L	$33 \times 23 \times 5$
Loaf Pan	$8 \times 4 \times 3$	1.5 L	$20 \times 10 \times 7$
	$9 \times 5 \times 3$	2 L	$23 \times 13 \times 7$
Round Layer Cake Pan	$8 \times 1 1/2$	1.2 L	20×4
	$9 \times 1 1/2$	1.5 L	23×4
Pie Plate	$8 \times 1 1/4$	750 mL	20×3
	$9 \times 1 1/4$	1 L	23×3
Baking Dish or Casserole	1 quart	1 L	—
	$1 1/2$ quart	1.5 L	—
	2 quart	2 L	—